W9-BEJ-667

© 2005 Christian Art Gifts, RSA
Christian Art Gifts Inc., IL, USA
Printed in China

Oct. 1, 2010

Today is the day that I received this journal from my friend, Tamara. I have been wanting to do some serious journaling and my friend gives me the opportunity.

Today was a special day because I was able to get my pier out of the lake BEFORE the weather turns cold next week. Thanks God for my nephew, Chris. With his help we got the job done. Therefore I can SWAN!

Tonight I had the privelege to have dinner with some of my dearest friends. We ate at Pesto's. Man the food was great Jeannie Tammy Tamara INTERRUPTION ————
My mother needed me to turn

The path of the just is as the shining light,
that shineth more and more unto the perfect day.
~ Proverbs 4:18

off the kitchen light.
Now Tammy Tamara
Jeannie and I went out
to dinner. Then Janine joined
us. It is really get to know
these girls as people. They
are really great people.

Oct. 2, 2010
Today we moved my
mother into Oak Wood
Manor. Rita, Moni, Darlene
Doug, Chris + Wyatt all
helped. Wyatt was a
really big help because
he has experience moving
furniture. Mom seemed
really fearfull this
morning. She even had
tears in her eyes before
we left my house. Once

Arise, shine; for thy light is come, and
the glory of the Lord is risen upon thee.
~ Isaiah 60:1

we got her to Oak Wood
and things started to
happen she seemed better.
I was feeling good about
everything until we walked
into Oak Wood and I
felt like I wanted to
cry like I'm doing
now.
        I'm happy that my
mother is in a safe place,
but I'm also saddened
by the fact that her life
is nearing an end and
she is not the kind of
mother that I could
ever go to for real help.
She has always been so
busy taking care of herself,
that there is nothing
left for taking care of

The name of the LORD is a strong tower:
the righteous runneth into it, and is safe.
~ Proverbs 18:10

anyone else.

Later this afternoon I went to Amish Acres with Laure. We ate dinner & saw the play Annie Get Your Gun.

It was a great performance and I really enjoyed myself. I really felt like there is a pecking order in our seating arrangements and I am not on the top. But the overall seating was good. A lot better than last year.

I hope my mother is happy at Oak Wood. At least she is in a safe, clean environment where she is no longer alone. She will be eating better and

"Blessed are the pure in heart: for they shall see God."
~ Matthew 5:8

will hopefully have a better quality of life.
    While she was staying with me I was able to observe something. My mother gets crabby pouty and ugly when she doesn't get her own way. She doesn't do anything but watch TV. She doesn't seem to comprehend drama shows. She wears the same clothes all the time. She could live on ice cream, cookies milk Arnold Palmer tea and beer. She does like her coffee in the morning. She is up off + on all night going to the bathroom. And it is not my fault

For the eyes of the Lord are over the righteous,
and His ears are open unto their prayers.
~ 1 Peter 3:12

that she cannot hear!

All in all I'm glad that I've had this time with her but I'm glad she is in her own place being cared for and entertained.

Under all the dirt and mess my mother does have some beautiful furniture. Maybe she will leave things uncovered and uncluttered.

I have tried to be a good daughter, even if being the daughter of Ruth has meant alot of work and responsibility for me. I sometimes feel like being the oldest I carry the weight

Blessed is every one that feareth the LORD; that walketh in His ways. For thou shalt eat the labour of thine hands: happy shalt thou be, and it shall be well with thee.

~ Psalm 128:1-2

of my dysfunctional family on my shoulders. Sometimes I cannot believe how messed up my family is. No one but me does anything to try to improve themselves and I have worked damned hard. I need to start putting all that work to good use and start enjoying my life more and working less. I need to just be responsible for myself and my life. I am going to work on creating my BEST LIFE!

The LORD is good to all: and His tender mercies are over all His works.
~ Psalm 145:9

Oct. 3, 2010

Today was a most interesting day. I spent most of the day reclaiming my house. I washed clothes, re-arranged my living room & spare room. I vacuumed washed floors & mowed the lawn. Finally around 4pm I showed & headed for moms.

On the way I called Margaret & we had a verbal exchange. I got so tired of listening to her whine and make excuses. I called to talk to her about mom and ask her to think about the family letting me move into moms house & I would sell my house & use the proceeds to renovate the house. Well she doesn't

Being confident of this very thing, that He which hath begun a good work in you will perform it until the day of Jesus Christ.

~ Philippians 1:6

want that to happen because she needs money. She doesn't have a job therefore she has no money. Well to have money you have to have a job to have a job you have to work to work you have to do things you don't want to do. Oh well Thank God I have a program a sponsor and program friends. I know it was a God thing when Emily called. Seems she has a sister like mine. My sponsor let me verbalize & vent. Then Emily called. and could emphasize with me. Emily also suggested I make an options list. Tomorrow

And of His fulness have all we received, and grace for grace.

~ John 1:16

I will begin work on my options list. And I am also going to write about my resentments toward Margaret.

Then my night was topped off with my conversation w/ Tamara. I got to thank her & tell her about what my journal birthday gift is doing for me. I have never had an "OFFICIAL" journal before and I plan to use this one.

Oct. 4, 2010

Today was an uneventful day with the exception of my new lawn furniture. My neighbor was throwing away some wrought Iron lawn

Oh that men would praise the LORD for His goodness, and for His wonderful works to the children of men! For He satisfieth the longing soul, and filleth the hungry soul with goodness.

~ Psalm 107:8-9

furniture. Four chair and a table. They are almost what I have been looking for all summer. The price is right — F.REE.

Also my niece, Megan called tonight. I miss her so much. She is such a wonderful girl. The reason I haven't heard from her is she is working at least 5 day a week now. She says she is paying her bills & saving for her cruise. I worry so about her. I want only the best life for my sweet niece. I need to be praying for her. I'll also be praying for Chris.

And we know that all things work together for good to them that love God, to them who are the called according to His purpose.

~ Romans 8:28

Oct. 5, 2010

Moving my mom into the assisted living facility is like riding a roller coaster. There are highs & there are lows. Tonight my mom asked me how long she was going to have to stay at Oak Woods. I didn't have the heart to say forever so I just said I did not know.

On the high side she seems to be communicating more and is able to carry on a conversation but there are times when I am fully aware of why we put her in Oak Wood.

For the LORD God is a sun and shield: the LORD
will give grace and glory: no good thing
will He withhold from them that walk uprightly.
~ Psalm 84:11

Oct. 12, 2010

Today I drove to S.B. for my extensive bloodtest but the promise. Dave was supposed to go before work & do his but he showed up at about the same time I was there. Too bad we are not talking maybe 2 this could have been avoided. I also thought it strange that the keys were in the truck. I used the truck late yesterday afternoon & I used the 2nd set of keys. Dave was not at work yesterday so I don't understand how the 1st set of keys got in the truck. My Mom and I bowled together tonight on the same alleys we had a great time. She won $32.00 in the 50-50.

For the LORD is good; His mercy is everlasting;
and His truth endureth to all generations.
~ Psalm 100:5

When I took her home she asked me to come up to her apartment. I promptly fell asleep. Mom seems to be doing alot better in the assisted living facility. She is more alert, more alive & more cordial. She served me orange juice while I was there.

The LORD taketh pleasure in them that fear Him, in those that hope in His mercy.

~ Psalm 147:11

Jan 27, 2011

Yesterday I told my OA sponsor that for the time being I am not going to attend OA meetings in particular the Monday nite meeting.

It was difficult for me to bring myself to tell her this but I believe it is the right thing to do. I plan to concentrate on my al-anon meeting + making up an exercise program.

I am going to miss my sponsor she has taught me so much. I really trusted her. Lately I have been feeling like she doesn't have

"If thou canst believe, all things are possible to him that believeth."
~ Mark 9:23

time for me and that is
one of the things that I
need most.

I really like having
a sponsor who can
talk the family disease
of alcoholism with me.
I just pray she will
not move back to Oklahoma
anytime soon.

April 11, 2011

Today I got my taxes
figured. Then I came
home and made phone
calls for my 1st PBR

Currently I have 4
people on my list I
also found out that
cousins Carol has a detached
retina and Frannie has
breast cancer. I also

Eye hath not seen, nor ear heard, neither have
entered into the heart of man, the things
which God hath prepared for them that love Him.

~ 1 Corinthians 2:9

found out that Ada's oldest son Mark has come home. These things are more important then ACN. My phone calling went very well and I'm looking forward to Wednesday nite. Now I gotta go pray.

Dec. 4, 2011

Today was a great day. I went to Jan's after work + played with Princess + Mindy while Jan + I talked. Then I called mom when I got home to get Ann's number. I called Ann + we talked for 15 mins. I asked her to go to the H.S. Choir concert

Behold, the eye of the LORD is upon them that
fear Him, upon them that hope in His mercy.
~ Psalm 33:18

didn't want to go — too late.
not's faling well. She's going
to Dr. tomorrow. I'll
call her afternoon
Next called Mary & Don
to see if they could go
can't sit in seats for
prolonged period. Nice
talk
Next called Laura. She
can go Wednesday nite.
I realized I need to put
myself out there to
connect w/ people.
Spent the rest of the nite
decorating, paying bills &
getting organized.

But my God shall supply all your need
according to His riches in glory by Christ Jesus.
~ Philippians 4:19

May 14, 2012

I feel great today! I have submitted a job application to Hormel. I don't know if I will get the job or not—the outcome is in God's hands. But at least I have tried.

I'm also proud of the fact that I was able to submit my resume and cover letter on line. I needed Kelly's help but at least I got the job done.

Tomorrow is Thursday and I am looking forward to my al-anon meeting in Portage.

I talked to both Wyatt and Chris today. Wyatt is suffering from a perferated ulcer. He'll be in Florida for

There are many devices in a man's heart;
nevertheless the counsel of the LORD, that shall stand.

~ Proverbs 19:21

2 more weeks. —
Chris has survived
Afganistan with Gods help.
I'm so glad he is getting out
of there! Praise God.

And therefore will the LORD wait, that He may
be gracious unto you, and therefore will He
be exalted, that He may have mercy upon you.
~ *Isaiah 30:18*

The LORD hath prepared His throne in the heavens;
and His kingdom ruleth over all.

~ *Psalm 103:19*

_____

Blessed be the God and Father of our Lord Jesus Christ, who hath
blessed us with all spiritual blessings in heavenly places in Christ.
~ Ephesians 1:3

_____

Thou wilt shew me the path of life: in Thy presence is fulness
of joy; at Thy right hand there are pleasures for evermore.

~ *Psalm 16:11*

_____

Mercy unto you, and peace, and love, be multiplied.
~ Jude 2

The blessing of the LORD, it maketh rich,
and He addeth no sorrow with it.

~ Proverbs 10:22

_____

Now the God of hope fill you with all joy and peace in believing,
that ye may abound in hope, through the power of the Holy Ghost.

~ Romans 15:13

God be merciful unto us, and bless us;
and cause His face to shine upon us.

~ Psalm 67:1

Cause me to hear Thy lovingkindness in the morning;
for in Thee do I trust: cause me to know the way
wherein I should walk; for I lift up my soul unto Thee.

~ Psalm 143:8

Cast thy burden upon the LORD, and He shall sustain
thee: He shall never suffer the righteous to be moved.

~ Psalm 55:22

_____

The LORD shall preserve thee from all evil: He shall
preserve thy soul. The LORD shall preserve thy going out and
thy coming in from this time forth, and even for evermore.

~ Psalm 121:7-8

Trust in the LORD with all thine heart; and lean
not unto thine own understanding. In all thy ways
acknowledge Him, and He shall direct thy paths.

~ Proverbs 3:5-6

_____

Rejoice evermore. Pray without ceasing.
In every thing give thanks: for this is the
will of God in Christ Jesus concerning you.
~ *1 Thessalonians 5:16-18*

_____

The path of the just is as the shining light,
that shineth more and more unto the perfect day.

~ Proverbs 4:18

_____

Arise, shine; for thy light is come, and
the glory of the Lᴏʀᴅ is risen upon thee.
~ *Isaiah 60:1*

The name of the Lord is a strong tower:
the righteous runneth into it, and is safe.
~ Proverbs 18:10

_____

"Blessed are the pure in heart: for they shall see God."
~ Matthew 5:8

_____

For the eyes of the Lord are over the righteous,
and His ears are open unto their prayers.

~ *1 Peter 3:12*

_____

Blessed is every one that feareth the LORD; that walketh
in His ways. For thou shalt eat the labour of thine hands:
happy shalt thou be, and it shall be well with thee.

~ Psalm 128:1-2

The LORD is good to all: and His tender
mercies are over all His works.

~ *Psalm 145:9*

_____

Being confident of this very thing, that He which hath begun
a good work in you will perform it until the day of Jesus Christ.
~ *Philippians 1:6*

And of His fulness have all we received, and grace for grace.

~ John 1:16

_____

Oh that men would praise the LORD for His goodness, and for
His wonderful works to the children of men! For He satisfieth
the longing soul, and filleth the hungry soul with goodness.

~ Psalm 107:8-9

And we know that all things work together for good to them that love God, to them who are the called according to His purpose.

~ Romans 8:28

_____

For the Lᴏʀᴅ God is a sun and shield: the Lᴏʀᴅ
will give grace and glory: no good thing
will He withhold from them that walk uprightly.

~ Psalm 84:11

For the LORD is good; His mercy is everlasting;
and His truth endureth to all generations.

~ Psalm 100:5

_____

The LORD taketh pleasure in them that
fear Him, in those that hope in His mercy.

~ Psalm 147:11

"If thou canst believe, all things are p   him that believeth."
~ *Mark 9:23*

Eye hath not seen, nor ear heard, neither have
entered into the heart of man, the things
which God hath prepared for them that love Him.

~ *1 Corinthians 2:9*

Behold, the eye of the L‍ord is upon them that
fear Him, upon them that hope in His mercy.

~ Psalm 33:18

_____

But my God shall supply all your need
according to His riches in glory by Christ Jesus.
~ *Philippians 4:19*

There are many devices in a man's heart;
nevertheless the counsel of the Lord, that shall stand.

~ Proverbs 19:21

_____

And therefore will the Lord wait, that He may
be gracious unto you, and therefore will He
be exalted, that He may have mercy upon you.
~ *Isaiah 30:18*

The LORD hath prepared His throne in the heavens;
and His kingdom ruleth over all.

~ *Psalm 103:19*

Blessed be the God and Father of our Lord Jesus Christ, who hath blessed us with all spiritual blessings in heavenly places in Christ.

~ Ephesians 1:3

Thou wilt shew me the path of life: in Thy presence is fulness
of joy; at Thy right hand there are pleasures for evermore.

~ Psalm 16:11

_____

Mercy unto you, and peace, and love, be multiplied.
~ Jude 2

The blessing of the LORD, it maketh rich,
and He addeth no sorrow with it.

~ Proverbs 10:22

_____

Now the God of hope fill you with all joy and peace in believing,
that ye may abound in hope, through the power of the Holy Ghost.

~ Romans 15:13

God be merciful unto us, and bless us;
and cause His face to shine upon us.

~ *Psalm 67:1*

_____

Cause me to hear Thy lovingkindness in the morning;
for in Thee do I trust: cause me to know the way
wherein I should walk; for I lift up my soul unto Thee.

~ Psalm 143:8

Cast thy burden upon the LORD, and He shall sustain
thee: He shall never suffer the righteous to be moved.

~ *Psalm 55:22*

_____

The LORD shall preserve thee from all evil: He shall preserve thy soul. The LORD shall preserve thy going out and thy coming in from this time forth, and even for evermore.

~ Psalm 121:7-8

_____

Trust in the LORD with all thine heart; and lean
not unto thine own understanding. In all thy ways
acknowledge Him, and He shall direct thy paths.

~ *Proverbs 3:5-6*

_____

Rejoice evermore. Pray without ceasing.
In every thing give thanks: for this is the
will of God in Christ Jesus concerning you.

~ *1 Thessalonians 5:16-18*

The path of the just is as the shining light,
that shineth more and more unto the perfect day.
~ Proverbs 4:18

_____

Arise, shine; for thy light is come, and
the glory of the Lᴏʀᴅ is risen upon thee.

~ Isaiah 60:1

The name of the LORD is a strong tower:
the righteous runneth into it, and is safe.

~ Proverbs 18:10

_____

"Blessed are the pure in heart: for they shall see God."
~ Matthew 5:8

For the eyes of the Lord are over the righteous,
and His ears are open unto their prayers.

~ 1 Peter 3:12

_____

Blessed is every one that feareth the Lord; that walketh
in His ways. For thou shalt eat the labour of thine hands:
happy shalt thou be, and it shall be well with thee.

~ Psalm 128:1-2

The LORD is good to all: and His tender
mercies are over all His works.

~ *Psalm 145:9*

_____

Being confident of this very thing, that He which hath begun
a good work in you will perform it until the day of Jesus Christ.
~ Philippians 1:6

And of His fulness have all we received, and grace for grace.
~ *John 1:16*

_____

Oh that men would praise the Lord for His goodness, and for
His wonderful works to the children of men! For He satisfieth
the longing soul, and filleth the hungry soul with goodness.

~ Psalm 107:8-9

And we know that all things work together for good to them that love God, to them who are the called according to His purpose.

~ Romans 8:28

_____

For the LORD God is a sun and shield: the LORD
will give grace and glory: no good thing
will He withhold from them that walk uprightly.
~ *Psalm 84:11*

For the LORD is good; His mercy is everlasting;
and His truth endureth to all generations.

~ Psalm 100:5

_____

The LORD taketh pleasure in them that
fear Him, in those that hope in His mercy.

~ *Psalm 147:11*

"If thou canst believe, all things are possible to him that believeth."
~ Mark 9:23

_____

Eye hath not seen, nor ear heard, neither have
entered into the heart of man, the things
which God hath prepared for them that love Him.
~ 1 Corinthians 2:9

Behold, the eye of the Lord is upon them that
fear Him, upon them that hope in His mercy.

~ Psalm 33:18

_____

But my God shall supply all your need
according to His riches in glory by Christ Jesus.
~ *Philippians 4:19*

There are many devices in a man's heart;
nevertheless the counsel of the LORD, that shall stand.
~ Proverbs 19:21

_____

And therefore will the LORD wait, that He may
be gracious unto you, and therefore will He
be exalted, that He may have mercy upon you.

~ Isaiah 30:18

The LORD hath prepared His throne in the heavens;
and His kingdom ruleth over all.

~ *Psalm 103:19*

_____

Blessed be the God and Father of our Lord Jesus Christ, who hath blessed us with all spiritual blessings in heavenly places in Christ.

~ *Ephesians 1:3*

Thou wilt shew me the path of life: in Thy presence is fulness
of joy; at Thy right hand there are pleasures for evermore.

~ Psalm 16:11

_____

Mercy unto you, and peace, and love, be multiplied.
~ Jude 2

The blessing of the Lord, it maketh rich,
and He addeth no sorrow with it.

~ Proverbs 10:22

_____

Now the God of hope fill you with all joy and peace in believing,
that ye may abound in hope, through the power of the Holy Ghost.

~ Romans 15:13

God be merciful unto us, and bless us;
and cause His face to shine upon us.

~ Psalm 67:1

_____

Cause me to hear Thy lovingkindness in the morning;
for in Thee do I trust: cause me to know the way
wherein I should walk; for I lift up my soul unto Thee.

~ Psalm 143:8

Cast thy burden upon the LORD, and He shall sustain
thee: He shall never suffer the righteous to be moved.

~ *Psalm 55:22*

_____

The LORD shall preserve thee from all evil: He shall
preserve thy soul. The LORD shall preserve thy going out and
thy coming in from this time forth, and even for evermore.

~ *Psalm 121:7-8*

Trust in the Lord with all thine heart; and lean
not unto thine own understanding. In all thy ways
acknowledge Him, and He shall direct thy paths.

~ Proverbs 3:5-6

_____

Rejoice evermore. Pray without ceasing.
In every thing give thanks: for this is the
will of God in Christ Jesus concerning you.
~ *1 Thessalonians 5:16-18*

The path of the just is as the shining light,
that shineth more and more unto the perfect day.

~ Proverbs 4:18

_____

Arise, shine; for thy light is come, and
the glory of the LORD is risen upon thee.
~ Isaiah 60:1

The name of the L ORD is a strong tower:
the righteous runneth into it, and is safe.
~ *Proverbs 18:10*

_____ .

_____
_____
_____
_____
_____
_____
_____
_____
_____
_____
_____
_____
_____
_____
_____
_____
_____
_____
_____
_____
_____
_____

"Blessed are the pure in heart: for they shall see God."
~ Matthew 5:8

For the eyes of the Lord are over the righteous,
and His ears are open unto their prayers.

~ *1 Peter 3:12*

_____

Blessed is every one that feareth the LORD; that walketh
in His ways. For thou shalt eat the labour of thine hands:
happy shalt thou be, and it shall be well with thee.

~ Psalm 128:1-2

The Lord is good to all: and His tender
mercies are over all His works.

~ Psalm 145:9

_____

Being confident of this very thing, that He which hath begun
a good work in you will perform it until the day of Jesus Christ.

~ *Philippians 1:6*

And of His fulness have all we received, and grace for grace.
~ *John 1:16*

_____

Oh that men would praise the Lord for His goodness, and for
His wonderful works to the children of men! For He satisfieth
the longing soul, and filleth the hungry soul with goodness.

~ Psalm 107:8-9

And we know that all things work together for good to them that love God, to them who are the called according to His purpose.

~ Romans 8:28

_____

For the LORD God is a sun and shield: the LORD
will give grace and glory: no good thing
will He withhold from them that walk uprightly.
~ Psalm 84:11

For the LORD is good; His mercy is everlasting;
and His truth endureth to all generations.

~ Psalm 100:5

_____

The Lord taketh pleasure in them that
fear Him, in those that hope in His mercy.
~ *Psalm 147:11*

"If thou canst believe, all things are possible to him that believeth."
~ Mark 9:23

_____

Eye hath not seen, nor ear heard, neither have
entered into the heart of man, the things
which God hath prepared for them that love Him.

~ *1 Corinthians 2:9*

Behold, the eye of the LORD is upon them that
fear Him, upon them that hope in His mercy.
~ *Psalm 33:18*

_____

But my God shall supply all your need
according to His riches in glory by Christ Jesus.
~ *Philippians 4:19*

There are many devices in a man's heart;
nevertheless the counsel of the LORD, that shall stand.
~ Proverbs 19:21

_____

And therefore will the Lord wait, that He may
be gracious unto you, and therefore will He
be exalted, that He may have mercy upon you.

~ Isaiah 30:18

The LORD hath prepared His throne in the heavens;
and His kingdom ruleth over all.

~ *Psalm 103:19*

_____

Blessed be the God and Father of our Lord Jesus Christ, who hath blessed us with all spiritual blessings in heavenly places in Christ.

~ Ephesians 1:3

Thou wilt shew me the path of life: in Thy presence is fulness
of joy; at Thy right hand there are pleasures for evermore.

~ Psalm 16:11

_____

Mercy unto you, and peace, and love, be multiplied.
~ *Jude 2*

The blessing of the LORD, it maketh rich,
and He addeth no sorrow with it.

~ Proverbs 10:22

_____

_____

_____

_____

_____

_____

_____

_____

_____

_____

_____

_____

_____

_____

_____

_____

_____

_____

_____

_____

_____

_____

Now the God of hope fill you with all joy and peace in believing,
that ye may abound in hope, through the power of the Holy Ghost.

~ Romans 15:13

God be merciful unto us, and bless us;
and cause His face to shine upon us.

~ Psalm 67:1

Cause me to hear Thy lovingkindness in the morning;
for in Thee do I trust: cause me to know the way
wherein I should walk; for I lift up my soul unto Thee.

~ Psalm 143:8

Cast thy burden upon the LORD, and He shall sustain
thee: He shall never suffer the righteous to be moved.

~ Psalm 55:22

The LORD shall preserve thee from all evil: He shall preserve thy soul. The LORD shall preserve thy going out and thy coming in from this time forth, and even for evermore.

~ *Psalm 121:7-8*

Trust in the LORD with all thine heart; and lean
not unto thine own understanding. In all thy ways
acknowledge Him, and He shall direct thy paths.

~ Proverbs 3:5-6

_____

Rejoice evermore. Pray without ceasing.
In every thing give thanks: for this is the
will of God in Christ Jesus concerning you.

~ 1 Thessalonians 5:16-18

The path of the just is as the shining light,
that shineth more and more unto the perfect day.
~ *Proverbs 4:18*

_____

Arise, shine; for thy light is come, and
the glory of the LORD is risen upon thee.
~ Isaiah 60:1

The name of the LORD is a strong tower:
the righteous runneth into it, and is safe.
~ *Proverbs 18:10*

_____

"Blessed are the pure in heart: for they shall see God."
~ Matthew 5:8

For the eyes of the Lord are over the righteous,
and His ears are open unto their prayers.
~ *1 Peter 3:12*

_____

Blessed is every one that feareth the Lord; that walketh
in His ways. For thou shalt eat the labour of thine hands:
happy shalt thou be, and it shall be well with thee.

~ Psalm 128:1-2

_____

_____
_____
_____
_____
_____
_____
_____
_____
_____
_____
_____
_____
_____
_____
_____
_____
_____
_____
_____
_____

The Lord is good to all: and His tender
mercies are over all His works.

~ *Psalm 145:9*

_____

Being confident of this very thing, that He which hath begun
a good work in you will perform it until the day of Jesus Christ.
~ *Philippians 1:6*

_____

_____

_____

_____

_____

_____

_____

_____

_____

_____

_____

_____

_____

_____

_____

_____

_____

_____

_____

_____

_____

_____

And of His fulness have all we received, and grace for grace.

~ John 1:16

_____

Oh that men would praise the LORD for His goodness, and for
His wonderful works to the children of men! For He satisfieth
the longing soul, and filleth the hungry soul with goodness.

~ Psalm 107:8-9

And we know that all things work together for good to them that
love God, to them who are the called according to His purpose.

~ *Romans 8:28*

_____

For the LORD God is a sun and shield: the LORD
will give grace and glory: no good thing
will He withhold from them that walk uprightly.
~ Psalm 84:11

For the Lord is good; His mercy is everlasting;
and His truth endureth to all generations.

~ Psalm 100:5

_____

The LORD taketh pleasure in them that
fear Him, in those that hope in His mercy.
~ *Psalm 147:11*

"If thou canst believe, all things are possible to him that believeth."

~ Mark 9:23

_____

Eye hath not seen, nor ear heard, neither have
entered into the heart of man, the things
which God hath prepared for them that love Him.

~ *1 Corinthians 2:9*

Behold, the eye of the Lord is upon them that
fear Him, upon them that hope in His mercy.

~ Psalm 33:18

_____

But my God shall supply all your need
according to His riches in glory by Christ Jesus.
~ Philippians 4:19

There are many devices in a man's heart;
nevertheless the counsel of the LORD, that shall stand.

~ Proverbs 19:21

And therefore will the LORD wait, that He may
be gracious unto you, and therefore will He
be exalted, that He may have mercy upon you.

~ Isaiah 30:18

The Lord hath prepared His throne in the heavens;
and His kingdom ruleth over all.
~ *Psalm 103:19*

_____

Blessed be the God and Father of our Lord Jesus Christ, who hath blessed us with all spiritual blessings in heavenly places in Christ.

~ *Ephesians 1:3*

Thou wilt shew me the path of life: in Thy presence is fulness
of joy; at Thy right hand there are pleasures for evermore.

~ Psalm 16:11

_____

Mercy unto you, and peace, and love, be multiplied.
~ *Jude 2*

The blessing of the LORD, it maketh rich,
and He addeth no sorrow with it.

~ *Proverbs 10:22*

_____

Now the God of hope fill you with all joy and peace in believing,
that ye may abound in hope, through the power of the Holy Ghost.

~ Romans 15:13

_____

_____
_____
_____
_____
_____
_____
_____
_____
_____
_____
_____
_____
_____
_____
_____
_____
_____
_____
_____
_____
_____
_____

God be merciful unto us, and bless us;
and cause His face to shine upon us.
~ Psalm 67:1

Cause me to hear Thy lovingkindness in the morning;
for in Thee do I trust: cause me to know the way
wherein I should walk; for I lift up my soul unto Thee.

~ Psalm 143:8

Cast thy burden upon the Lord, and He shall sustain
thee: He shall never suffer the righteous to be moved.

~ Psalm 55:22

_____

The LORD shall preserve thee from all evil: He shall
preserve thy soul. The LORD shall preserve thy going out and
thy coming in from this time forth, and even for evermore.

~ Psalm 121:7-8

Trust in the LORD with all thine heart; and lean
not unto thine own understanding. In all thy ways
acknowledge Him, and He shall direct thy paths.

~ Proverbs 3:5-6

_____

Rejoice evermore. Pray without ceasing.
In every thing give thanks: for this is the
will of God in Christ Jesus concerning you.
~ *1 Thessalonians 5:16-18*

The path of the just is as the shining light,
that shineth more and more unto the perfect day.

~ Proverbs 4:18

_____

Arise, shine; for thy light is come, and
the glory of the Lord is risen upon thee.
~ *Isaiah 60:1*

The name of the LORD is a strong tower:
the righteous runneth into it, and is safe.

~ Proverbs 18:10

_____

"Blessed are the pure in heart: for they shall see God."
~ Matthew 5:8

For the eyes of the Lord are over the righteous,
and His ears are open unto their prayers.

~ 1 Peter 3:12

_____

Blessed is every one that feareth the LORD; that walketh
in His ways. For thou shalt eat the labour of thine hands:
happy shalt thou be, and it shall be well with thee.

~ *Psalm 128:1-2*

_____

_____
_____
_____
_____
_____
_____
_____
_____
_____
_____
_____
_____
_____
_____
_____
_____
_____
_____
_____
_____
_____
_____
_____

The LORD is good to all: and His tender
mercies are over all His works.

~ Psalm 145:9

_____

Being confident of this very thing, that He which hath begun
a good work in you will perform it until the day of Jesus Christ.

~ Philippians 1:6

And of His fulness have all we received, and grace for grace.

~ *John 1:16*

_____

Oh that men would praise the Lord for His goodness, and for
His wonderful works to the children of men! For He satisfieth
the longing soul, and filleth the hungry soul with goodness.

~ *Psalm 107:8-9*

And we know that all things work together for good to them that love God, to them who are the called according to His purpose.

~ Romans 8:28

_____

For the LORD God is a sun and shield: the LORD
will give grace and glory: no good thing
will He withhold from them that walk uprightly.
~ *Psalm 84:11*

For the Lord is good; His mercy is everlasting;
and His truth endureth to all generations.

~ Psalm 100:5

_____

The LORD taketh pleasure in them that
fear Him, in those that hope in His mercy.

~ *Psalm 147:11*

"If thou canst believe, all things are possible to him that believeth."
~ *Mark 9:23*

_____

Eye hath not seen, nor ear heard, neither have
entered into the heart of man, the things
which God hath prepared for them that love Him.
~ *1 Corinthians 2:9*

Behold, the eye of the Lord is upon them that
fear Him, upon them that hope in His mercy.

~ Psalm 33:18

_____

But my God shall supply all your need
according to His riches in glory by Christ Jesus.
~ *Philippians 4:19*

There are many devices in a man's heart;
nevertheless the counsel of the LORD, that shall stand.
~ Proverbs 19:21

_____

And therefore will the LORD wait, that He may
be gracious unto you, and therefore will He
be exalted, that He may have mercy upon you.

~ *Isaiah 30:18*

The LORD hath prepared His throne in the heavens;
and His kingdom ruleth over all.

~ Psalm 103:19

_____

Blessed be the God and Father of our Lord Jesus Christ, who hath
blessed us with all spiritual blessings in heavenly places in Christ.
~ Ephesians 1:3

Thou wilt shew me the path of life: in Thy presence is fulness of joy; at Thy right hand there are pleasures for evermore.

~ Psalm 16:11

_____

Mercy unto you, and peace, and love, be multiplied.
~ *Jude 2*

The blessing of the Lord, it maketh rich,
and He addeth no sorrow with it.

~ Proverbs 10:22

_____

Now the God of hope fill you with all joy and peace in believing,
that ye may abound in hope, through the power of the Holy Ghost.
~ Romans 15:13

God be merciful unto us, and bless us;
and cause His face to shine upon us.

~ Psalm 67:1

_____

Cause me to hear Thy lovingkindness in the morning;
for in Thee do I trust: cause me to know the way
wherein I should walk; for I lift up my soul unto Thee.
~ Psalm 143:8

Cast thy burden upon the LORD, and He shall sustain
thee: He shall never suffer the righteous to be moved.

~ *Psalm 55:22*

The LORD shall preserve thee from all evil: He shall preserve thy soul. The LORD shall preserve thy going out and thy coming in from this time forth, and even for evermore.

~ Psalm 121:7-8

Trust in the LORD with all thine heart; and lean
not unto thine own understanding. In all thy ways
acknowledge Him, and He shall direct thy paths.

~ Proverbs 3:5-6

_____

Rejoice evermore. Pray without ceasing.
In every thing give thanks: for this is the
will of God in Christ Jesus concerning you.
~ *1 Thessalonians 5:16-18*

The path of the just is as the shining light,
that shineth more and more unto the perfect day.

~ Proverbs 4:18

_____

Arise, shine; for thy light is come, and
the glory of the Lord is risen upon thee.
~ *Isaiah 60:1*

The name of the LORD is a strong tower:
the righteous runneth into it, and is safe.
~ *Proverbs 18:10*

_____

"Blessed are the pure in heart: for they shall see God."
~ *Matthew 5:8*

For the eyes of the Lord are over the righteous,
and His ears are open unto their prayers.

~ 1 Peter 3:12

_____

Blessed is every one that feareth the Lord; that walketh in His ways. For thou shalt eat the labour of thine hands: happy shalt thou be, and it shall be well with thee.

~ Psalm 128:1-2

The Lord is good to all: and His tender
mercies are over all His works.

~ Psalm 145:9

_____

Being confident of this very thing, that He which hath begun
a good work in you will perform it until the day of Jesus Christ.

~ Philippians 1:6

_____

_____
_____
_____
_____
_____
_____
_____
_____
_____
_____
_____
_____
_____
_____
_____
_____
_____
_____
_____
_____
_____
_____

And of His fulness have all we received, and grace for grace.

~ *John 1:16*

_____

Oh that men would praise the Lᴏʀᴅ for His goodness, and for His wonderful works to the children of men! For He satisfieth the longing soul, and filleth the hungry soul with goodness.

~ Psalm 107:8-9

And we know that all things work together for good to them that love God, to them who are the called according to His purpose.

~ Romans 8:28

_____

For the Lord God is a sun and shield: the Lord
will give grace and glory: no good thing
will He withhold from them that walk uprightly.

~ Psalm 84:11

"If thou canst believe, all things are possible to him that believeth."
~ Mark 9:23

_____

Eye hath not seen, nor ear heard, neither have
entered into the heart of man, the things
which God hath prepared for them that love Him.

~ 1 Corinthians 2:9

Behold, the eye of the LORD is upon them that
fear Him, upon them that hope in His mercy.

~ *Psalm 33:18*

_____

But my God shall supply all your need
according to His riches in glory by Christ Jesus.
~ *Philippians 4:19*

There are many devices in a man's heart;
nevertheless the counsel of the LORD, that shall stand.

~ Proverbs 19:21

_____

And therefore will the Lord wait, that He may
be gracious unto you, and therefore will He
be exalted, that He may have mercy upon you.
~ Isaiah 30:18

The Lord hath prepared His throne in the heavens;
and His kingdom ruleth over all.

~ *Psalm 103:19*

_____

Blessed be the God and Father of our Lord Jesus Christ, who hath blessed us with all spiritual blessings in heavenly places in Christ.

~ Ephesians 1:3

Thou wilt shew me the path of life: in Thy presence is fulness of joy; at Thy right hand there are pleasures for evermore.

~ Psalm 16:11

_____

Mercy unto you, and peace, and love, be multiplied.
~ Jude 2

The blessing of the LORD, it maketh rich,
and He addeth no sorrow with it.

~ Proverbs 10:22

_____

Now the God of hope fill you with all joy and peace in believing,
that ye may abound in hope, through the power of the Holy Ghost.
~ Romans 15:13

God be merciful unto us, and bless us;
and cause His face to shine upon us.

~ Psalm 67:1

Cause me to hear Thy lovingkindness in the morning;
for in Thee do I trust: cause me to know the way
wherein I should walk; for I lift up my soul unto Thee.

~ *Psalm 143:8*

Cast thy burden upon the LORD, and He shall sustain
thee: He shall never suffer the righteous to be moved.

~ Psalm 55:22

_____

The Lord shall preserve thee from all evil: He shall
preserve thy soul. The Lord shall preserve thy going out and
thy coming in from this time forth, and even for evermore.

~ Psalm 121:7-8

Trust in the Lᴏʀᴅ with all thine heart; and lean
not unto thine own understanding. In all thy ways
acknowledge Him, and He shall direct thy paths.

~ Proverbs 3:5-6

_____

Rejoice evermore. Pray without ceasing.
In every thing give thanks: for this is the
will of God in Christ Jesus concerning you.

~ 1 Thessalonians 5:16-18

_____

The path of the just is as the shining light,
that shineth more and more unto the perfect day.

~ Proverbs 4:18

_____

Arise, shine; for thy light is come, and
the glory of the Lord is risen upon thee.

~ Isaiah 60:1

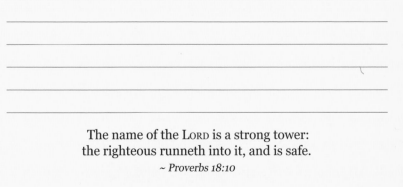

The name of the LORD is a strong tower:
the righteous runneth into it, and is safe.

~ Proverbs 18:10

_____

"Blessed are the pure in heart: for they shall see God."
~ Matthew 5:8

For the eyes of the Lord are over the righteous,
and His ears are open unto their prayers.

~ 1 Peter 3:12

_____

Blessed is every one that feareth the Lᴏʀᴅ; that walketh
in His ways. For thou shalt eat the labour of thine hands:
happy shalt thou be, and it shall be well with thee.

~ Psalm 128:1-2

The Lord is good to all: and His tender
mercies are over all His works.

~ Psalm 145:9

_____

Being confident of this very thing, that He which hath begun
a good work in you will perform it until the day of Jesus Christ.

~ Philippians 1:6

And of His fulness have all we received, and grace for grace.

~ John 1:16

_____

Oh that men would praise the Lᴏʀᴅ for His goodness, and for His wonderful works to the children of men! For He satisfieth the longing soul, and filleth the hungry soul with goodness.

~ Psalm 107:8-9

And we know that all things work together for good to them that love God, to them who are the called according to His purpose.

~ Romans 8:28

_____

For the LORD God is a sun and shield: the LORD
will give grace and glory: no good thing
will He withhold from them that walk uprightly.

~ *Psalm 84:11*

For the LORD is good; His mercy is everlasting;
and His truth endureth to all generations.

~ Psalm 100:5